Breathe In, Breathe Out
LEARNING ABOUT YOUR LUNGS

WRITTEN BY PAMELA HILL NETTLETON
ILLUSTRATED BY BECKY SHIPE

Thanks to our advisers for their expertise, research, and advice:
Angela Busch, M.D., All About Children Pediatrics, Minneapolis, Minnesota

Susan Kesselring, M.A., Literacy Educator
Rosemount-Apple Valley-Eagan (Minnesota) School District

PICTURE WINDOW BOOKS
MINNEAPOLIS, MINNESOTA

Managing Editor: Bob Temple
Creative Director: Terri Foley
Editor: Kristin Thoennes Keller
Editorial Adviser: Andrea Cascardi
Copy Editor: Laurie Kahn
Designer: Melissa Voda
Page production: The Design Lab
The illustrations in this book were rendered digitally.

Picture Window Books
5115 Excelsior Boulevard
Suite 232
Minneapolis, MN 55416
1-877-845-8392
www.picturewindowbooks.com

Printed in the United States of America.

Library of Congress Cataloging-in-Publication Data
Nettleton, Pamela Hill.
  Breathe in, breathe out: learning about your lungs / by Pamela Hill
Nettleton ; illustrated by Becky Shipe.
      p. cm. — (The amazing body)
Summary: An introduction to the lungs and how they function.
  ISBN 1-4048-0254-1 (Reinforced Library Binding)
1. Lungs—Juvenile literature. [1. Lungs.] I. Shipe, Becky, 1977– ill. II. Title.
  QP121 .N44 2004
    612.2—dc22   2003018187

Take a deep breath. Have you ever thought about where air goes once it's inside your body?

The air you breathe in goes into your lungs.
They are sort of like two pink balloons.

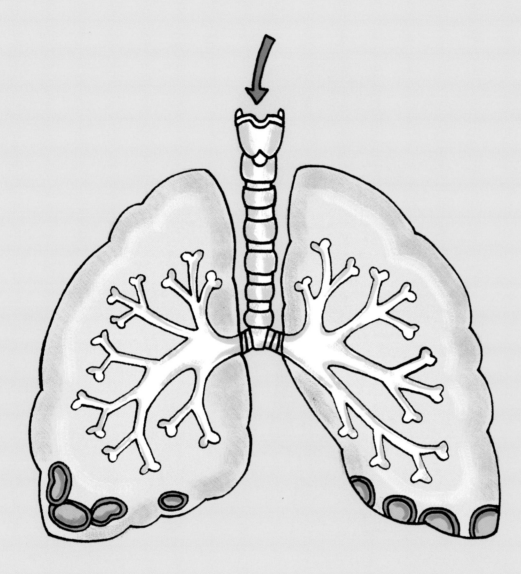

Your lungs fill up with air when you breathe in.
They send out air when you breathe out.

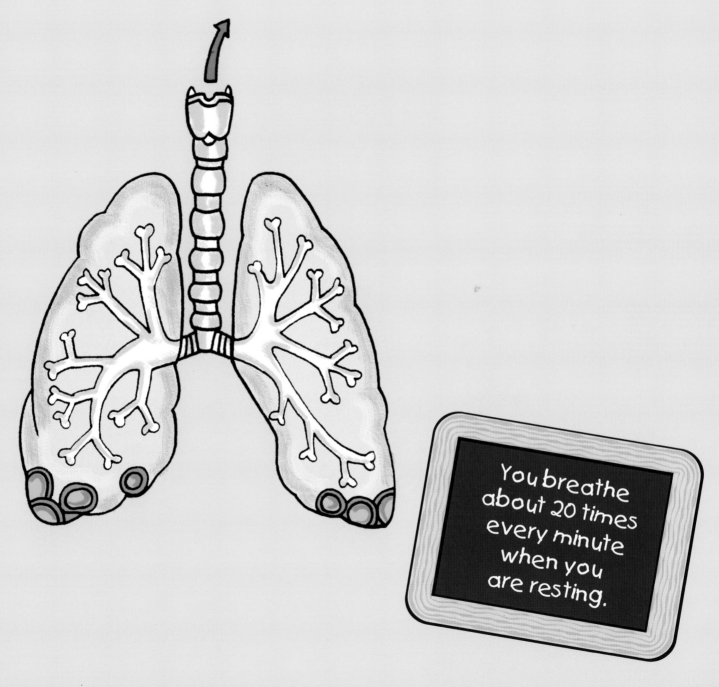

You breathe
about 20 times
every minute
when you
are resting.

Your lungs are in your chest. Your rib cage protects them. That's a good thing.

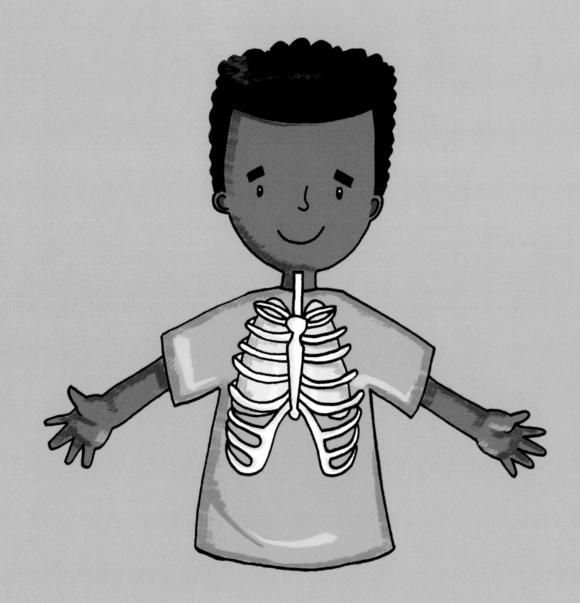

Your lungs are very important. Lungs bring a gas called oxygen into your body. You need this gas to live.

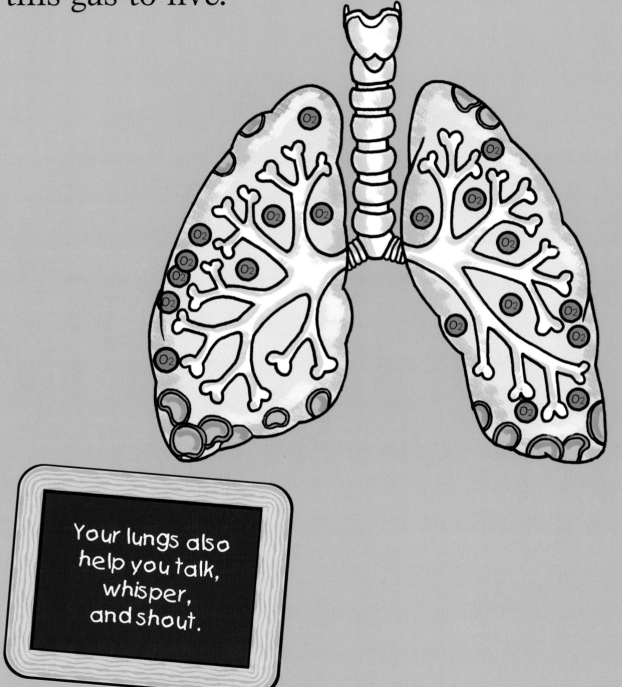

Your lungs also help you talk, whisper, and shout.

Whoosh! Air enters your body through your nose or mouth. Your throat collects the air and passes it to a tube called the windpipe, or trachea.

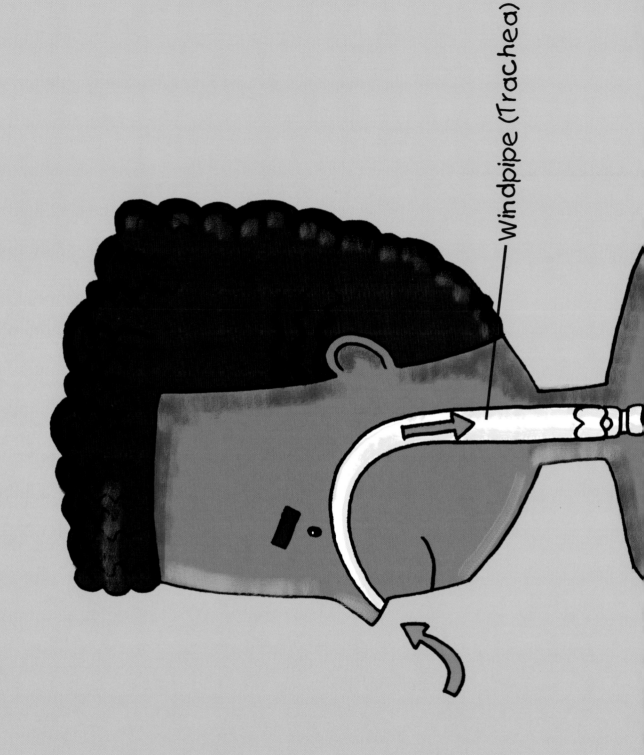

Windpipe (Trachea)

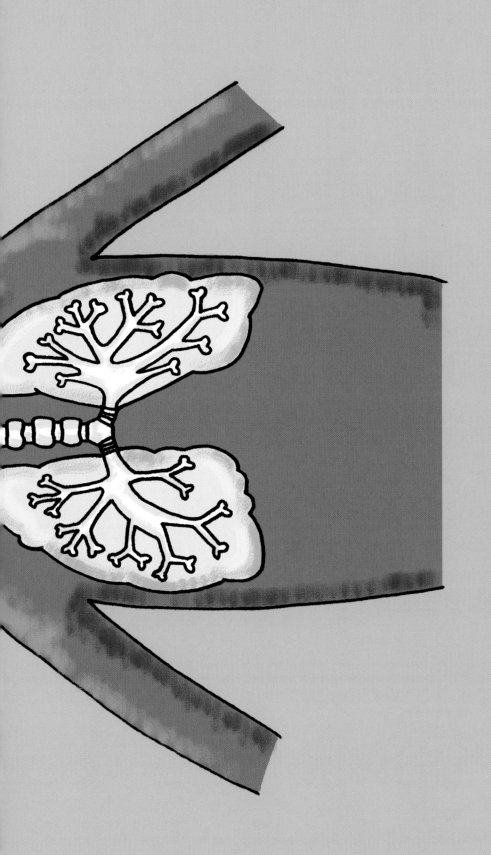

The windpipe splits into two tubes. Each tube leads to one of your lungs.

Inside your lungs, there are soft little tubes called bronchial tubes. Air moves through these tubes.

The bronchial tubes have a sticky liquid called mucus in them. Mucus catches dust, germs, and other things. You get rid of these things when you cough, clear your throat, swallow, and sneeze. Ah-choo!

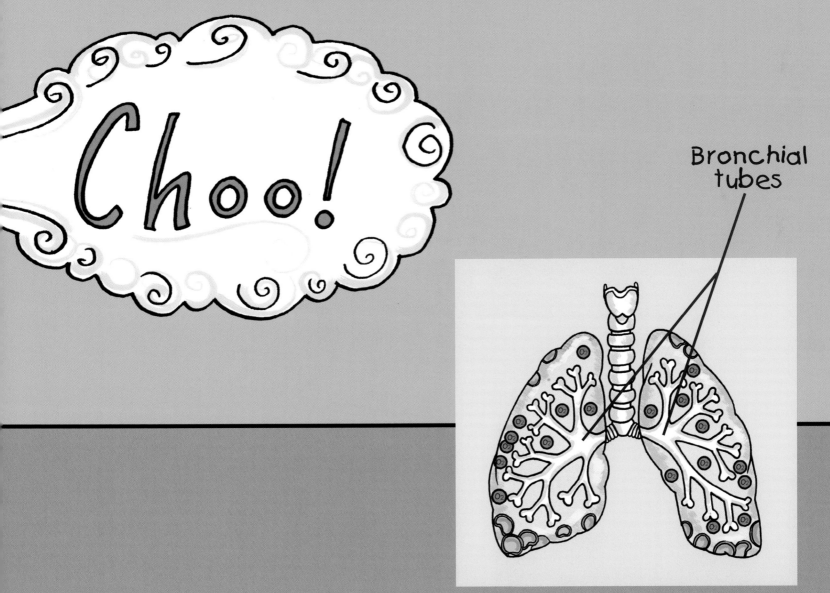

Bronchial tubes

The smallest sections of your bronchial tubes are called the bronchioles. If you were to draw them, they would look a little like the branches of a tree.

At the end of the bronchioles are lots of little air sacs, or bubbles. These air sacs are called alveoli. The alveoli are the final stop for your air.

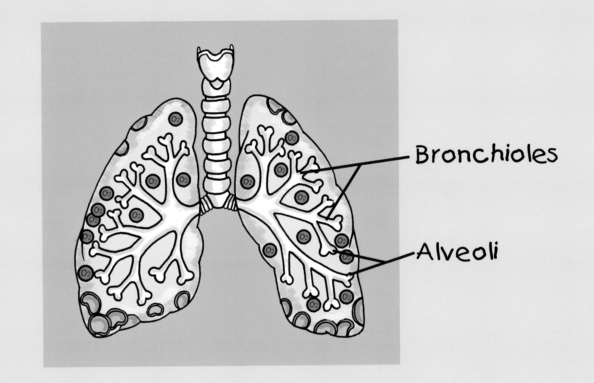

Bronchioles

Alveoli

Your blood passes back and forth through the walls of the alveoli. The blood picks up fresh oxygen from the air you breathe and drops off carbon dioxide. Your body doesn't need carbon dioxide, so you get rid of it by breathing out.

Then, your blood rushes to all your body parts, bringing oxygen and energy.

When blood is full of carbon dioxide, it is bluish purple. When it has fresh oxygen, it is bright red.

When you breathe, a special muscle called the diaphragm moves underneath your lungs. It helps push air out and pull air in. Take a deep breath and feel your diaphragm move down. It gives your lungs lots of room.

Lungs love exercise! Run hard and feel how your lungs change the speed of your breathing to help you.

Blow air back out again. You can feel your diaphragm bounce back up.

Some people have asthma. Asthma is a disease that makes it hard to breathe.

Playing or working hard can make asthma worse. Cold weather also can make it worse.

People with asthma may carry inhalers. Inhalers bring medicine to their lungs to help them breathe better.

Has anyone ever told you to take a deep breath? Maybe that person was trying to help you feel better. Maybe he or she was trying to help you calm down.

Taking a deep breath helps give your body the fresh oxygen it needs. So breathe!

The worst thing you can do to your lungs is to smoke. Smoking makes it harder to breathe. Smoking can cause cancer in your lungs. Don't smoke!

THE LUNGS

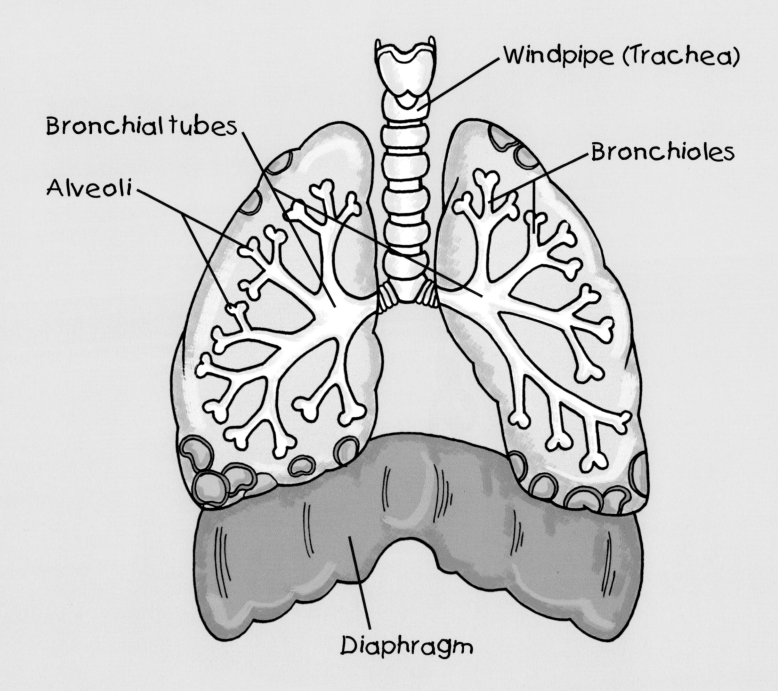

Windpipe (Trachea)

Bronchial tubes

Bronchioles

Alveoli

Diaphragm

TAKE A DEEP BREATH!

Do the following tests. Then compare your answers with a friend.

1. Count how many breaths it takes you to fill a balloon.
2. Count how many seconds you can hold your breath.
3. Count how many breaths you take in one minute when resting.
4. Run in place for two minutes. Then count how many breaths you take in one minute after running.

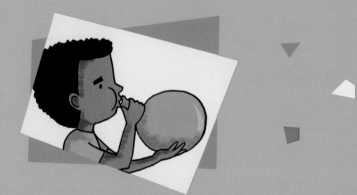

TOOLS OF THE TRADE

When you go to your doctor, he or she listens to your lungs. Your doctor uses a special instrument called a stethoscope. This tool makes the tiny sounds inside your lungs sound loud. The doctor puts the stethoscope's flat disk on your skin. He or she listens to your heart, your lungs, and other important body parts. These sounds tell a doctor a lot about what's going on inside you. With the help of the stethoscope, a doctor can tell the difference between healthy and sick sounds.

GLOSSARY

alveoli (AL-vee-oh-leye)—little air sacs inside your lungs where blood picks up oxygen

bronchial tubes (BRONG-kee-uhl TOOBZ)—tiny tubes inside your lungs. Air passes through these tubes.

bronchioles (BRONG-kee-ohlz)—the smallest sections of your bronchial tubes

carbon dioxide (KAR-buhn dye-OK-side)—the part of the air your body gets rid of

diaphragm (DYE-uh-fram)—the muscle under your lungs that moves as you breathe

oxygen (OK-suh-juhn)—the part of the air your body needs

rib cage (RIB KAYJ)—a set of curved bones that protects your heart and lungs

stethoscope (STETH-uh-skope)—a special tool your doctor uses to listen to your lungs

windpipe (WIND-pipe)—the tube in your throat that brings air from your mouth and nose to your lungs. Trachea is another word for windpipe.

TO LEARN MORE

At the Library

Ballard, Carol. *Lungs*. Chicago: Heinemann Library, 2003.

Furgang, Kathy. *My Lungs*. New York: PowerKids Press, 2001.

Stille, Darlene. *The Respiratory System*. New York: Children's Press, 1997.

On the Web

Fact Hound offers a safe, fun way to find Web sites related to this book. All of the sites on Fact Hound have been researched by our staff. *http://www.facthound.com*

1. Visit the Fact Hound home page.
2. Enter a search word related to this book, or type in this special code: 1404802541.
3. Click the FETCH IT button.

Your trusty Fact Hound will fetch the best sites for you!

INDEX